PARAPSYCHOLOGY
Facts and a Medical Approach

By

Nawar Sabah Ajwad

Förlag: BoD - Books on Demand, Stockholm, Sverige
Tryck: BoD - Books on Demand, Norderstedt, Tyskland
ISBN: 978-91-7785-374-9

"Life is like music, it must be composed by ear, feeling and instinct, not by rule. Nevertheless one had better know the rules, for they sometimes guide in doubtful cases, though not often"

Paracelsus

Contents

<u>Introduction</u>

The word parapsychology consists of three parts, Para is from Greek and means beside and psycho which means mind or sole and logy which means science. The word was used for the first time in 1889 by philosopher Max Dessoir.

Parapsychology is the science of many phenomena that are considered today as ambiguous and vague because of the inability of modern science to prove the parapsychological phenomena scientifically.

If we look at parapsychology as a science then it should have its laws in science in order to make it a solid science. Unfortunately until now parapsychology do not have clear and agreeable laws despite many hundreds years of research in this field of study.

The reason for that is the absence of the advanced technological devices that can measure the very subtle types of energies or vibrations that characterize each parapsychological phenomenon.

If there are phenomena that we, with the use of modern science can not explain, then logically there must be a reasonable and satisfying explanation for each of those phenomena. The parapsychological phenomena that we see or hear or feel which do not fit in a scientific law do not lose its value as a truth does not lose its value although it is hidden or undiscovered. Therefore the mission of the genuine researcher and every one who seeks the truth in this field of study is to look after the reasons that made such phenomena to take place. It is almost rarely that researchers use technological devices and instruments to help them discovering the hidden nature of the parapsychological phenomena. Therefore there are no parapsychological laws in the present time that match the standard of any other science other than parapsychology. The word paranormal usually used in parapsychology and I do not favor the use of it because I consider that each phenomena must be normal because it has happened and it will happen again and again. We hear it, see it, feel it and we have absolutely no way to ignore it and therefore it should be normal despite that we can not prove it scientifically.

For all reasons that I have mentioned so far, parapsychology is sometimes called pseudoscience, i.e. it is not a real science which I think it is a false name, simply because if we can not prove it scientifically we do not need to claim that it is not a real science because the facts and the truths are out there and they only need someone to discover them. In another word, they exist and they will do exist until they can be discovered.

We all belong to the nature on this earth and the nature has its natural secrets that are not yet discovered by researchers and scientist. When Isaac Newton for example discovered the law of gravity, no one could believe there would be a mathematical calculation that can formulate the gravity law until it was done and no one at that time could imagine that there was a unique formulation that can explain why objects fall towards the earth when they are in the space because it was so natural experience that it was hard to think what was the reason that make the objects fall. When the magician does his tricks, we enjoy them and we become surprised and astonished how he accomplishes his work. We know that he cheat us in certain way but we do not know how. The magician here is the nature with its laws and we, the audience, are the seekers of the truth in each phenomenon that we do not realize and understand well.

We as people have an internal desire in our unconsciousness to believe in things that are proved by the tools of science such as physics, mathematics and medicine but we do not have the psychological mechanism in our unconsciousness to accept the unproven things despite their existence in our life. If a phenomenon does exist but it is not proved yet scientifically, most of the ordinary people neglect it and do not think about it as a fact. The people need a scientific proof that a certain phenomenon is correct in order to be believed by them despite the fact that the phenomenon exist and it needs only to be proved like every discovery in the history of science. The proof is existing potentially but it is not found yet and that does not mean that the proof for many parapsychological phenomena can not be discovered.

During the history of research in parapsychology, certain researchers tried to prove a certain parapsychological phenomenon by only utilizing statistics, i.e. how many times an agent can do a parapsychological phenomenon in controlled conditions and that is not enough to have the whole picture of the phenomenon if we really want to understand it in a satisfying level. We need for example to understand why a phenomenon occurs and the reasons behind its occurrence. We need to know the physiological and physical mechanism of such phenomena and the quantum or metaphysical mechanisms if there are such mechanisms that can explain certain phenomena. We need also a deep understanding of the human aura which is the biological and natural field that surrounds the human body that consists of many intermingled layers.

Parapsychology have a very wide range of aspects and in order to understand them all we need a wide range of qualified abilities in many subjects in science.

When we try to explain something new in science we usually try to make a theory or a rational explanation that fit in the previous well known scientific laws but if we miss the advanced technological instruments in measuring the different aspects of the new phenomena then we try to explain the new and the unknown phenomena in what is called scientific models. Scientific models are based on scientific and logical facts that are reasonable and can be proved scientifically in the future.

In this book I will try to give facts and for the first time, solid models to my explanation and interpretation to the mysterious and the ambiguous parapsychological phenomena that has not been proved yet by science. It is an attempt to explore parapsychology scientifically.

This is not a treatment or diagnostic book but a try to understand the parapsychological phenomena from a medical point of view.

Clairvoyance

Clairvoyance means "clear vision" and it is the extra ordinary ability for rare individuals to see objects and events in the present, past and the future. Retrocognition and premonition are the terms used for clairvoyance in the past and the future respectively.

For the usual individuals the regions in the brain that are responsible for the interpretation of visual impulses and visual images from the outside of the human body are called striate and extra striate visual cortex areas. The striate area of the cortex of the human brain is dealing with the existing of the object's photo while extra striate area of the human brain cortex is dealing and processing features like shape, color and size. For the rare gifted individuals with clairvoyance, the striate and extra striate regions of the brain cortex are unique and developed in the way that makes them (the neurons in the regions and their branching and synapsis) very sensitive to many factors. The two regions can go beyond the time and space boundaries to experience facts, events and objects and make them available to the two visual regions in the brain.

If we take a simple look at the time as a factor in determining the type of clairvoyance whatever it is in the future, the present or the past we can see that the time is not a real factor as we understand it but only a category for the clairvoyance. We can not change time naturally but only theoretically. Most of the clairvoyants that predict the future, events in the present or the past have absolutely no ide how they do that. They just do it!

Sometimes they succeed in their mission and sometimes they fail because clairvoyance needs many environmental conditions to be a successful process if the clairvoyant is talented and trusted one. We need here to define destiny in order to be able to take a step near the clairvoyance. Destiny is everything that happens to a person or an object despite the external known events to the human beings. At the moment of the child birth, the universal force play a major factor in his life and that because of the unseen forces that the planets radiate to the earth continuously. Most of that forces are gravity forces. It is the mixed forces of the planets as a whole that affect the newly born baby's nervous system. The nervous system of the human beings is a very sensitive system at the birth of the baby and is affected permanently by the mixture of the planet's forces at the time of birth. Planet's forces reflect itself on the human body by the mean of the human aura that surrounds the human body. Planet forces become a part of the human aura at its basic structure and I call it birth human aura. We know that a healthy human aura is very necessary to keep the human body in a healthy state. The outflow of the human aura from the body goes to the cosmos and vice versa, i.e. the inflow of the human aura from the cosmos goes to the inside of the body. Both ways are mediated through the chakra system in the human body.

The clairvoyant uses the cosmos as a source of information about someone to predict the present event of his or her life because such information is available for everybody on earth but no one is able to sense the information. It is only sensible for the very rare part of the population who we call them clairvoyants.

Psychokinesis

Psychokinesis as a word consists of two parts and from Greek, psycho which means soul or mind and kinesis which means movement. It is the extra ordinary ability for rare individuals to move objects at distance without the use of any known physical methods. It we look at the psychokinesis closer we can find that it is puzzled and it is an ambiguous phenomena. How can an individual without using his hands or any part of his body be able to move certain objects without interfering with the subject physically? Well, it sounds magical indeed for the first time but for those who studied the human aura very well, they can find a reasonable answer for their big question, how?

We know that the human aura is the biological field that surrounds the human body and that it consists of many intermingled layers of different names, energies and vibrations.

The most powerful field in the human aura is the astral field which is characterized by its various continuously moving colored vibrational energies that indicate the quality of the human health depending on which color that can be seen mostly in the human aura.

We can imagine a model that can fit in psychokinesis phenomena and which can explain how the and why this phenomena occur naturally.

The most studied object in psychokinesis is the dice. The individual that have the psychokinetic ability tries to influence the dice in order to make a certain face to show up when it stops moving. As we know that aura flow in and out of the human body continuously depending on the emotional and thinking status of the person. Well, at the moment when the dice is rolling, the individual that has the psychokinesis ability has the desire that a certain and a chosen face in his mind will show up. That psychological desire is very important in psychokinesis because it induces the release of many neurotransmitters in the human brain especially dopamine and serotonin, both are responsible for the excitement we experience in casino when we gamble!

These known neurotransmitters have both positive and negative feedback from the environment. For example, a specific type of perfume will stimulate or inhibit the release of these neurotransmitters and depending on its type and smell, it can block or enhance the psychokinesis phenomenon.

In another word the unconscious must not be disturbed or effected by certain factors that reduce the psychokinesis ability.

We mentioned before that the aura has two directions, in and out of the body. In psychokinesis the flow of the human aura out of the human body is the most interesting part in order to have a model that can explain psychokinesis. The outflow of the human aura from the human body is originated from the nervous system and the endocrine glands but in psychokinesis the outflow from the nervous system that is the major factor rather than the endocrine system because the nervous system is much faster in controlling the human aura. All the desire that an individual has to make the dice to stop at a certain face is interpreted and stored in the outflow stream of the human aura from the human body and anything that affects the desire will ultimately affect the result of the psychokinesis and the result that we obtain in each psychokinesis experiment. As we mentioned before, the main field which is responsible for psychokinesis is the astral field or what is called sometime astral body because it is the most powerful field in physical term that can control the object and make it move as the individual who is gifted with the psychokinetic ability wishes.

But how can the astral field moves different objects and which mechanism lies behind that "unphysical" movement?

The model that can explain that is the ability of the astral field to shape itself, take the color and the dimensions of the objects that are movable by psychokinesis. In another word, the original astral field that is radiated from the human body builds the movable object of the same material of the astral field, i.e. of certain level of vibrating energy that can been seen by clairvoyants and some types of cameras which are specialized for that purpose, i.e. too see the human aura.

After building a "copy" of the movable object from the astral field, that "copy" of the object which is made of the astral field reaches the dice through space (the dice here is an example of a movable object) and it will be a process of fitting or matching of both the copy and the original object. It matches the original object physically and dimensionally.

Because the copy of the dice and its material which is from the astral field of the human aura are both under the control of the human desire and the unconscious then the message from the brain cortex can be transmitted to the unconscious and then to the astral field of the human aura. This is the main pathway of the outflow of the human aura in general from the inside of the human body to the outside.

Then when the copy from the astral body and the original dice or any movable object fits and matches each other the process of the magical thing begins! The dice for example here will follow the desire that the copy of the dice bear which is initiated from the individual brain and his unconscious.

The favorable and the already chosen face of the dice will appear upwards after the dice has stopped from moving. No one certainly has been able to see the whole of this process in casino or somewhere else because our natural abilities to see things are limited as human beings.

Telepathy

Telepathy consists of two words, tele from Greek which means far away and pathein which means to have been affected by something.

Telepathy is defined as the ability of one person's mind to transmit thoughts or feelings to a second person's mind without using a well known physical method of transmission like the voice or any other known method. The mind of the sender or the agent is sending the thoughts and feelings consciously and the percipient receives the thoughts and the feelings unconsciously. Those people in population who are capable of telepathy are rare and those who have both way of transmission, i.e. they have the ability to send and also to receive the information (both thoughts and feelings) are very rare in the population.

There are two main types of telepathy concerning the time, latent telepathy and precognitive telepathy.

Latent telepathy is the type of telepathy where there is a gap in time between the start of transmission of the thought and or the feeling and the start of receiving that feeling and or thought whereas precognitive telepathy is the type of telepathy where the percipient receive the thought or the feeling of another person that are in the future, i.e. before they occur.

There is another classification of telepathy. It can be classified to gamma and kappa telepathy.

Gamma telepathy is the type of telepathy where the percipient receive extra sensory information (thought or feeling) from an agent. Kappa telepathy is the type of telepathy where the agent by its psi gamma can change motor parts of the percipient's nervous system or the whole nervous system including the brain.

If we think logically, then there must be a medium by which the thought or the feeling is transmitted through the space. The only known existing medium is either the air or the ether. The air is excluded because the telepathy is not like the voice that needs the air in order to be transmitted. The ether is not a quite good example as a medium for transmission. The mental field which is part of the human aura that surrounds the human body is a good medium for transmission of thoughts while in the case of feelings transmission, the astral body is a good medium.

And again it is only a model for explanation the parapsychological phenomenon because we do not have the enough advanced instruments to measure other mediums in the space.

We know that the aura that surrounds the human body is about many feet in depth and if the agent and recipient are existing near each other, that make the telepathic effects more visible and more clear. But we know that there are telepathic persons whom telepathic ability extend much more than many feet. In reality, there are telepathic persons whom their telepathic abilities can exceed many miles and their telepathic abilities still precise and intensive despite the percipient and the agent are separated from each other by many miles. Those are the masters in telepathic abilities and they are not many in the whole world.

Out of Body Experience

Out of body experience is a quite unique parapsychological phenomenon. It means that the person "leave" his human physical body and travelling everywhere in the world around. The travelling copy of the human body is called the astral double and the phenomenon is sometimes called astral projection. Notice that the astral double is something other than the astral body or astral field that is part of the human aura.

This phenomenon can occur spontaneously at any time of the individual's life time or induced by certain meditation that help the body goes in a very relaxing mode. The astral double during its travelling in places that the person chose when he is alert and awake continue to be connected to the physical human body through what is called the silver cord. This cord is very important to keep the person alive and it is very difficult to be damaged or cut. The other "world" that the person experiences during out of body experience OBE is very comfortable and lucid. Most of people that experienced OBE have said that and wanted to do it again.

If the physical human body that lie usually in bed is awakened by someone else or heard a loud voice then spontaneously the astral double return to its human physical body and the person becomes awake. The silver cord is for the safety of the person. There are no statistic that shows that there has happened a case where the silver cord is cut and the person dies, therefore astral travelling is very safe and can be done if the person follow certain types of mental and meditative exercises.

Many neuroscientists believe that over stimulation of the temporal lobe of the brain lead to out of body experiences and that can make sense because temporal lobe is responsible for the processing of the sensory input like visual and auditory input and that can make the person live in an OBE. The temporal lobe is also responsible for the long term memory and therefore the persons who experience OBE can remember their travelling outside their human physical body after returning to the physical body.

In the meditative state one can stimulate temporal lobe to the level of excitation which enables the person to experience OBE.

But what is the thing that is leaving the physical body? No clear and solid answer in psychic research history can explain that but we believe that it is the consciousness of the human mind that isolates itself from the physical body.

Near death experience

Near death experience or NDE is a similar phenomenon to OBE in that the individual experience leaving the physical body but the phenomenon is more emotionally intense. The individual has a feeling of bliss and comfort. Most of the individuals that experienced NDE describe as if they are moving throw a tunnel towards the light at the end of the tunnel. At the end of the tunnel they encounter the beloved ones and many divine characters.

The data that the researchers in this field of study receive are very rare and therefore this work is still in its infancy.

Certain studies show that deoxygenated blood or the lack of blood flow to the neurons, the nerve cells of the brain, is the key factor in experiencing NDE. If that is the case then a dying neurons are losing their vitality and function during NDE. That can lead us to the look closer to the consciousness of the mind or the human being as whole. If we consider that the consciousness is like the mass in physics, i.e. it can not disappear, then we should consider that the consciousness of the human being perhaps should go to another place after the death of the human brain. Now we consider the consciousness as a unique unit or thing that can be separated from the human being after its death. In fact the human brain shuts down or limits the consciousness in many people because of the somatic obstacles that the human body is characterized with and the individual's consciousness is at its highest level is when the consciousness is free from the physical human body.

Some Terms Used in Parapsychology

Extra sensory perception

The term was first used in the 1930s and covers telepathy, clairvoyance, psychokinesis and retrocognition.

Psi

The term was first used in 1942 and it identifies paranormal processes. The two main types of Psi are Psi gamma (extra sensory perception) Psi kappa (paranormal action; psychokinesis).
It also describes the anomalous outcomes.

Psitron

*A particle that is hypothesized to travel without frictional loss of energy
and carrying psi information physically to affect a real mass like the
individual's neurons to produce telepathy.*
Receiver

*An equivalent word to recipient and it indicates the acquisition of
telepathic information by an individual.*

Sender

*An equivalent word to agent and it indicates the sending of telepathic
information by an individual.*

Second sight

A concept that usually refers to the supernatural and to the individuals who have the psychic ability.

Scrying

A term used for the techniques that are used to get paranormal impressions. The methods that are used in scrying are several. They include staring into a crystal ball, pool of water, tea leaves and so on. Those practices can form images or non-pathological hallucinations at the person who is scrying.

Synchronicity

A term coined by Carl Jung with Pauli Wolfgang, 1955 which refers to a causal but a meaningful coincidence. Derived from the Greek, synchronos, syn- "with", chronos, "time".

Transpersonal Consciousness (TC)

A type of altered state of consciousness in which the awareness of the person is lost in, or identified with, an awareness of the whole world or other life form and it is induced by meditation.

Sitting

An interview between a medium and deceased people usually with one person or a small number of people. Also termed a "seance."

Subliminal

A term used to observe events occurring beneath the threshold of the conscious awareness.

Supraliminal

A term used to observe events occurring above the "threshold" level of conscious awareness.

Divination

A term used to refer to the acquiring of paranormal information by the use of different practices such as scrying, palmistry, I Ching and so on.

Ectoplasm

A word that describes the externalization of a physical substance out of the body of physical mediums.

The limbic system

This chapter deals with structures and functions that are under the term The "limbic system." The limbic system consists of cingulate gyrus, hippocampal formation, the septal nuclei and the amygdala.

These parts are regarded as the substance of emotions and subconscious processes, in contrast with the cognitive, conscious processes that are located in the neocortex. Sometimes it is called "the emotional brain" in order to describe these regions. Parts of the neocortex are implicating in processing of emotions- the prefrontal cortex and the insula.

Cell groups in the basal forebrain (including the nucleus accumbens) are densely interconnected with both limbic structures and the neocortex, and these cells groups participate in emotional and cognitive processing.

The amygdala (the amygdaloid nucleus) is located in the temporal lobe of the human brain. The amygdala is a complex of subnuclei, each with a distinctive internal structure, neurotransmitters and connections.

The afferent connections of the amygdala concerning the corticomedial nuclei are mostly from the olfactory bulb, the septal nuclei, the hypothalamus and the intralaminar thalamic nuclei.
These connections transmit information about taste and painful stimuli.
The basolateral nuclei receive signals from many thalamic nuclei, the prefrontal cortex, parts of the temporal lobes and the cingulate gyrus.
The lateral nucleus receives all sensory information.
While efferent connections of the amygdala connected mostly to hypothalamus. The amygdala also sends nerve fibers to some parts of the cortex that do not project back, especially to the inferotemporal visual areas. The hippocampal formation (the entorhinal area and the subuculum) and the septal nuclei receive some fibers from amygdala too. The projections to the basal nucleus can include activation of the EEG (arousal and increased attention). There are also fibers that arise from amygdala to various brain stem nuclei, such as PAG, parts of the reticular formation and parasympathetic cranial nerve nuclei. These connections together with the hypothalamus are important for the autonomic and somatic expression of emotions.

From higher association areas (Perirhinal cortex) there is connection with the amygdala. The amygdala then sends connections with the lateral hypothalamus which in turn sends connection to medulla oblongata which regulate the autonomic nervous system. Amygdala sends also nerve fibers to basal forebrain (Bed nucleus of stria terminalis) which in turn sends nerve fibers to PVN lobe in hypothalamus which connects median eminence and sends the nerve impulse further to anterior lobe of pituitary gland and an endocrine hormone (cortisol) are released to the blood stream.

Damage of the amygdala can affect the person in many ways. The person shows signs of tameness, i.e. the loss of aggressiveness and defensive reaction. In another word, the person shows deficiency in fight and flight reaction. After bilateral removal of the amygdala, the person shows also a reduction in behavioral expression of emotions. The vision stimuli of dangerous things will not trigger an adequate reaction of fight and flight reaction. These symptoms can be explained by the absent of connections from the amygdala with the hypothalamus and the brain stem autonomic and somatic motor centers (among them the PAG).

While stimulation of the basolateral nuclear group of the amygdala produces arousal and signs of increased attention.

The autonomic functions of the human being are influenced by cerebral cortex via the amygdala, the hippocampal formation and the septal nuclei which in turn influence the hypothalamus and brain stem nuclei.

The cingulate gyrus projects to the hippocampal formation, the septal nuclei and to the amygdala. All the last three regions have connections to the hypothalamus.

The hippocampus on the other hand has two way connections with different cortical association areas. The hippocampus has also direct and indirect connections with the structures of the limbic system (the amygdala, septal nuclei and cingulate gyrus.)

When the limbic system is at its highest level of healthy functionality the parapsychological phenomena used to be at its highest rate of occurrence. We can see that this happens only when the conscious awareness and the unconsciousness are in a typical harmony and they do not conflict each other. This will allow the human aura to flow very easily through the whole human body. Most of the people that have paranormal abilities are very healthy because any blockage of the human feelings will block the ability. We can see that the limbic system is very important not because it is of value to the human feelings but also because it is connected to the outer stimuli like vision, hearing and smell. It is very difficult to have a "pure" unconsciousness, i.e. the conflict between the consciousness and the unconsciousness is almost absent. The human ability to achieve the extra ordinary is depending largely on the feelings of the person. Most of the people who perform parapsychological phenomena are usually happy people and very alert in contrast to sad people whom their unconscious are filled with anxiety. The latter used not to have any parapsychological performance. We focus here on the external stimuli for the limbic system, i.e. the vision, the hearing and the smell. Those factors can affect the parapsychological abilities in tremendous ways. Any interruption in the limbic system by these three factors can lead to imbalance which can in turn lead to the failure of the agent to succeed in the performance of his extra ordinary achievements. A clear mind is very important in this case because every single internal or external stimulus can lead to a bias in the data that are received by the parapsychologist.

Therefore most of the experiments in parapsychology do not reveal the true nature of the phenomenon or its results just because the agent or the person who performs the parapsychological experiment do not feel safe or he is uncomfortable and that has its negative effect on the limbic system that has a major role in all parapsychological phenomenon.

Whenever there is a discussion about the extra ordinary abilities, i.e. paranormal abilities, we should mention the nature of the brain as a very advanced and complicated unit. We can say that the person is talented and with that we mean that the structure and the function of the brain are in its best favorable organization that enhances the occurrence of the paranormal phenomenon. The brain and specifically the limbic system is constructed of certain regions that are developed in a specific way which are suitable for the occurrence of the paranormal phenomenon. This development of these regions is located in the neurotransmitters that they release continuously. The type of those neurotransmitters that are released from the neurons, the amount of each neurotransmitter and the location of release in the brain are all factors that make the paranormal phenomena occur in reality and make the individuals having the ability of such extra ordinary abilities. Another factor that is very important is that the branching of the neurons is very suitable to enhance the parapsychological phenomenon. The ability of the neurons, the nerve cells, to make branches is called neuroplasticity.

For example the striate and extra striate visual areas have all these developmental factors that are mentioned above in order to make the person a clairvoyant. Therefore the micro anatomy of the talented persons in parapsychological phenomena have talented brains that are extra ordinary compared to the usual persons.

The human genome, i.e. all the genes in the chromosomes inside the cells play a crucial rule in the developed abilities. These genes expressed themselves during the growth of the individual to make many proteins and inside and outside the human cells. These proteins participate in the building of the neuronal components. People with parapsychological abilities have genes in their chromosomes that are specific for each of the *parapsychological phenomenon. So the person who has psychokinesis ability has psychokinesis genes and a person who has out of body experience (OBE) ability has OBE genes and so on.*

Some of these genes express themselves early in life and therefore we can see that a child can show extra ordinary abilities and some of the genes express themselves later in life and in a gradual way, therefore the parapsychological phenomenon become more and more intense with time or it becomes intense or quite enough for observation depending on the type of the gene in concern.